T0334486

grace

★ colour

★ reflect

★ rest

grace

☆ colour

☆ reflect

☆ rest

MONARCH BOOKS

Oxford UK, and Grand Rapids, USA

This edition published by Monarch Books
an imprint of
Lion Hudson plc
Wilkinson House, Jordan Hill Road,
Oxford OX2 8DR, England
Email: monarch@lionhudson.com
www.lionhudson.com/monarch

ISBN 978 0 85721 809 4

Acknowledgments

Unless otherwise stated, Scripture quotations taken from the Holy Bible, New International Version Anglicised. Copyright © 1979, 1984, 2011 Biblica, formerly International Bible Society. Used by permission of Hodder & Stoughton Ltd, an Hachette UK company. All rights reserved. "NIV" is a registered trademark of Biblica. UK trademark number 1448790.
Scriptures quotations marked KJV taken from The Authorized (King James) Version. Rights in the Authorized Version are vested in the Crown. Reproduced by permission of the Crown's patentee, Cambridge University Press.
Scriptures quotations marked GNB are from the Good News Bible © 1994 published by the Bible Societies/HarperCollins Publishers Ltd UK, Good News Bible© American Bible Society 1966, 1971, 1976, 1992. Used with permission.
Scripture quotations marked ESV are from The Holy Bible, English Standard Version® (ESV®) copyright © 2001 by Crossway, a publishing ministry of Good News Publishers. All rights reserved.

A catalogue record for this book is available from the British Library.

Printed and bound in Slovenia, January 2017, LH48

JOY IS PRAYER;

JOY IS STRENGTH …

JOY IS A NET OF LOVE

BY WHICH YOU CAN CATCH SOULS.

Mother Teresa

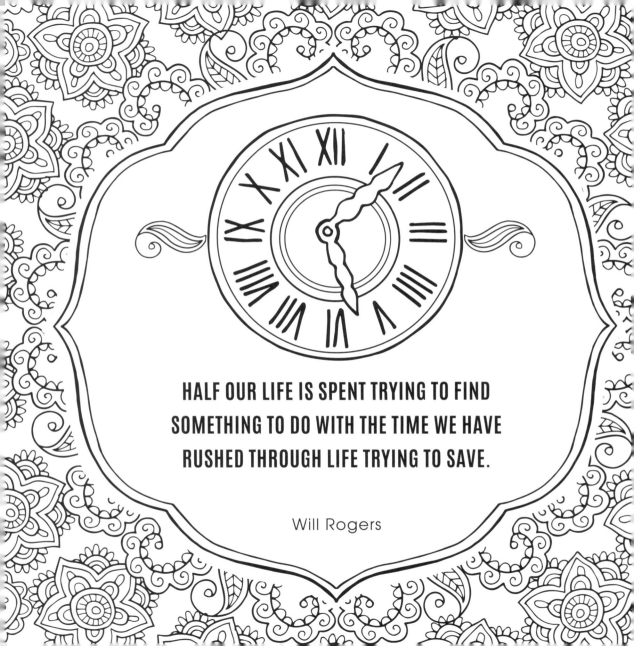

HALF OUR LIFE IS SPENT TRYING TO FIND
SOMETHING TO DO WITH THE TIME WE HAVE
RUSHED THROUGH LIFE TRYING TO SAVE.

Will Rogers

slower living

Busy. Stressed. I rush through the day, not taking the time to enjoy what I'm doing. Even when I spend time with loved ones I keep checking my smartphone.

Could I do things differently? Could I learn to live more slowly? To nourish my soul, to cherish my loved ones and to relish my blessings?

Don't you know that your body
is the temple of the Holy Spirit?

1 Corinthians 6:19 (GNB)

O taste and see that the LORD is good: blessed is the man that trusteth in him.

Psalm 34:8 (KJV)

☆ How can I cherish my loved ones?

....
....
....
....
....

☆ How have I been blessed?

....
....
....
....
....
....

☆ What does it mean that my body is a temple of the Holy Spirit?

....

....

....

....

....

....

☆ What do I enjoy?

....

....

....

....

....

....

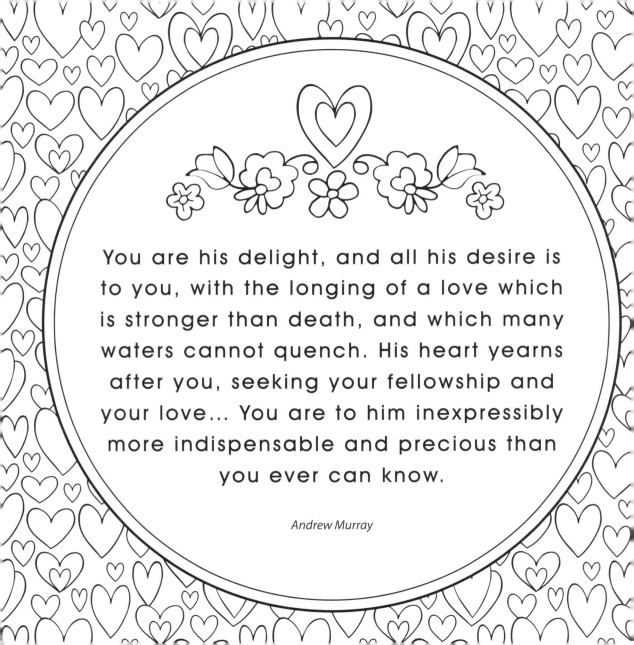

You are his delight, and all his desire is to you, with the longing of a love which is stronger than death, and which many waters cannot quench. His heart yearns after you, seeking your fellowship and your love... You are to him inexpressibly more indispensable and precious than you ever can know.

Andrew Murray

Loved

Precious. Cherished. Appreciated. That's what I am, that's what you are: God himself loves us. Feel free to check that in the Bible! He doesn't love us for our good behaviour or intellect, our considerate nature or beauty, but because he is our Father, who has created us. Do we accept his love?

I TRUST IN THE MERCY OF GOD
FOR EVER AND EVER.

Psalm 52:8 (KJV)

The Lord your God is with you;
his power gives you victory.
The Lord will take delight in you,
and in his love he will give you new life.
He will sing and be joyful over you.

Zephaniah 3:17 (GNB)

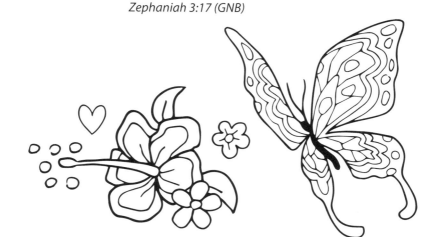

☆ In what way has it been difficult to see myself as God's precious child?

....
....
....
....
....
....

☆ What does it mean to me that I am loved?

....
....
....
....
....
....

☆ In what ways do I trust in God's love?

....
....
....
....
....
....

☆ What does God's love enable me to do?

....
....
....
....
....
....

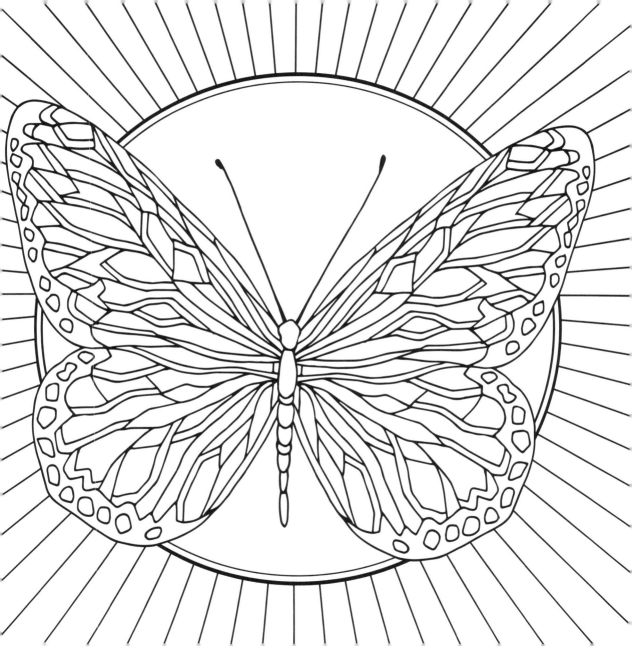

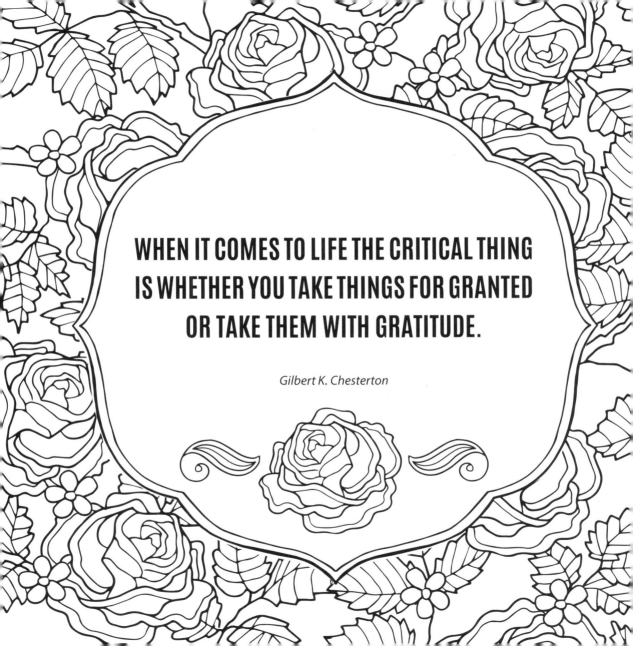

WHEN IT COMES TO LIFE THE CRITICAL THING
IS WHETHER YOU TAKE THINGS FOR GRANTED
OR TAKE THEM WITH GRATITUDE.

Gilbert K. Chesterton

Gratitude

Beautiful moments are like shining stars, and gratitude searches for the stars in every day. Gratitude is enjoying what has been given to me, and accepting goodness with a glad heart. The good that others have given to me, but also everything that God provides.

Gratitude is like physical fitness, it can be trained. I want to look for the good in each day, although it may be hard to find. I enjoy it and thank God for it.

And let the peace of God rule in your hearts,
to which also you were called in one body;
and be thankful.

Colossians 3:15

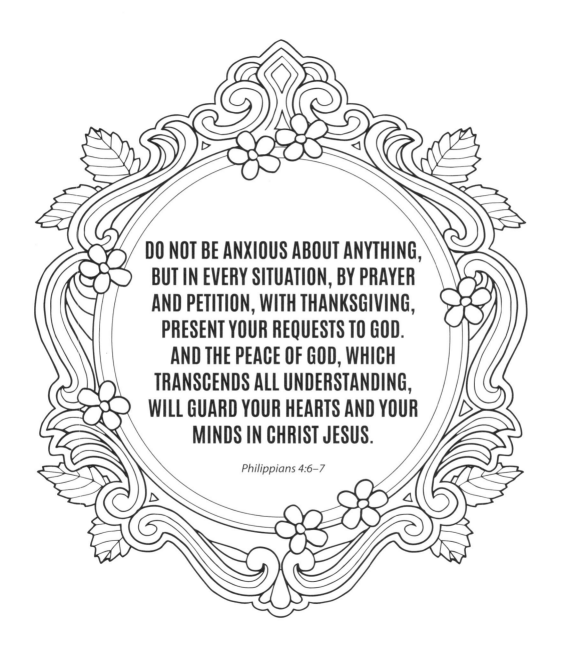

DO NOT BE ANXIOUS ABOUT ANYTHING,
BUT IN EVERY SITUATION, BY PRAYER
AND PETITION, WITH THANKSGIVING,
PRESENT YOUR REQUESTS TO GOD.
AND THE PEACE OF GOD, WHICH
TRANSCENDS ALL UNDERSTANDING,
WILL GUARD YOUR HEARTS AND YOUR
MINDS IN CHRIST JESUS.

Philippians 4:6–7

☆ What was good today?

....
....
....
....
....
....

☆ What did I enjoy about the past week?

....
....
....
....
....
....

☆ What can I thank the people around me for?

....

....

....

....

....

....

☆ What can I thank God for?

....

....

....

....

....

....

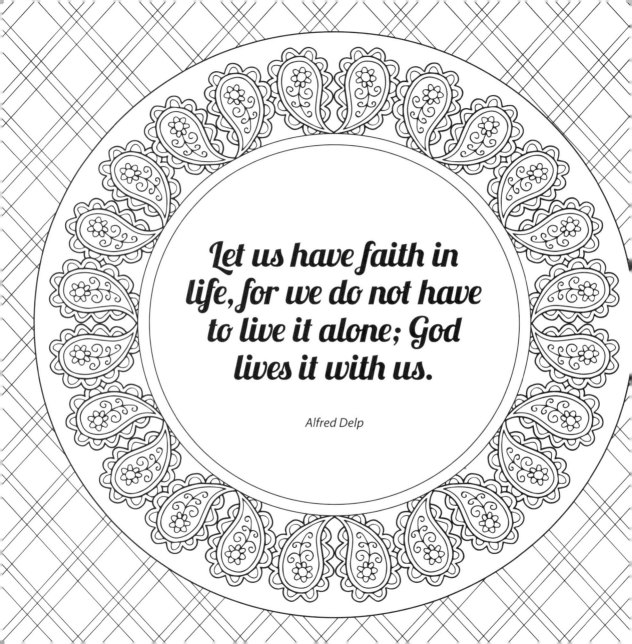

Let us have faith in life, for we do not have to live it alone; God lives it with us.

Alfred Delp

Trust

I like to sort things out all by myself. It makes me feel independent. Strong. But it also makes me insecure and worried: am I making the right decisions? Isn't there something I'm forgetting?

In the storms – both big and small – of my life I keep discovering I cannot make it on my own. I need people – family, friends. And above all, I need God. Every week, many churches affirm: "Our help is in the name of the Lord, the maker of heaven and earth, who always keeps his promises; whose love is eternal and who completes the work he has begun." (Psalm 124:8, 146:6, 138:8) Do I dare put my trust in Him?

Leave all your worries with him, because he cares for you.

1 Peter 5:7 (GNB)

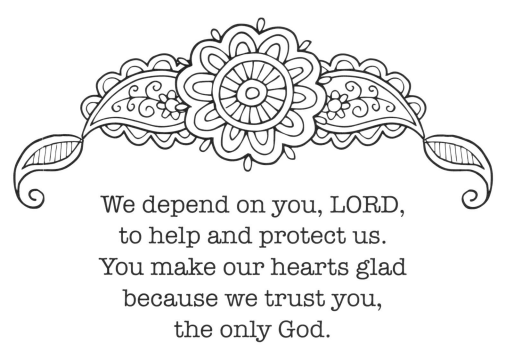

We depend on you, LORD,
to help and protect us.
You make our hearts glad
because we trust you,
the only God.

Psalm 33:20–21 (GNB)

☆ What concerns am I still carrying around?

....

....

....

....

....

....

☆ In what things do I need a little help, support, comfort, or strength?

....

....

....

....

....

....

☆ Who or what do I trust implicitly?

....
....
....
....
....
....

☆ In what ways have I experienced God's faithfulness?

....
....
....
....
....

The bow cannot be always bent without
fear of breaking. Repose is as needful
to the mind as sleep to the body...
Rest time is not waste time.
It is economy to gather fresh strength.

Charles Haddon Spurgeon

catching your breath

I spend all day running around. Work, appointments, obligations, exercise and housekeeping – until I've filled in every single hour. Could I find some time to contemplate or go for a silent walk? Could I free up a day in order to catch my breath?

Breathing space – repose after work – is part of God's plan. After making the heavens and the earth, God himself rested on the seventh day. Could I rest with him; at his feet?

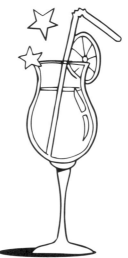

The Israelites are to observe the Sabbath. It will be a sign between me and the Israelites forever, for in six days the Lord made the heavens and the earth, and on the seventh day he rested and was refreshed.

Exodus 31:16-17

But Jesus often withdrew
to lonely places and prayed.

Luke 5:16

☆ How do I balance rest and work in my life?

....
....
....
....
....
....

☆ What wearies me?

....
....
....
....
....
....

☆ What pastimes do not really relax me?

....

....

....

....

....

....

☆ Where can I catch my breath?

....

....

....

....

....

....

If you want to build a ship,
don't drum up people to collect
wood and don't assign them tasks
and work, but rather teach them
to long for the endless immensity
of the sea.

Attributed to Antoine de Saint-Exupéry

longing

What is my 'endless immense sea'? What do I long for? What are my dreams? What motivates me? And how does that influence what I do? The Bible paints a picture of a heavenly life with God. A life filled with love and harmony, without tears, without war. How could longing for that life lead me today?

How lovely is your dwelling place,
Lord Almighty!
My soul yearns, even faints,
for the courts of the Lord;
my heart and my flesh cry out
for the living God.

Psalm 84:1–2

God's dwelling is with people,
and he will dwell with them,
and they will be his people,
and God himself will be with them
as their God. He will wipe away from
them every tear from their eyes.
Death will be no more; neither
will there be mourning, nor crying,
nor pain, any more. The first
things have passed away.

Revelation 21:3-4

☆ What are the desires of my heart?

....
....
....
....
....
....

☆ Who shares my dreams?

....
....
....
....
....
....

☆ What longings have I let go of?

....

....

....

....

....

....

☆ What is God's role in what I long for?

....

....

....

....

....

....

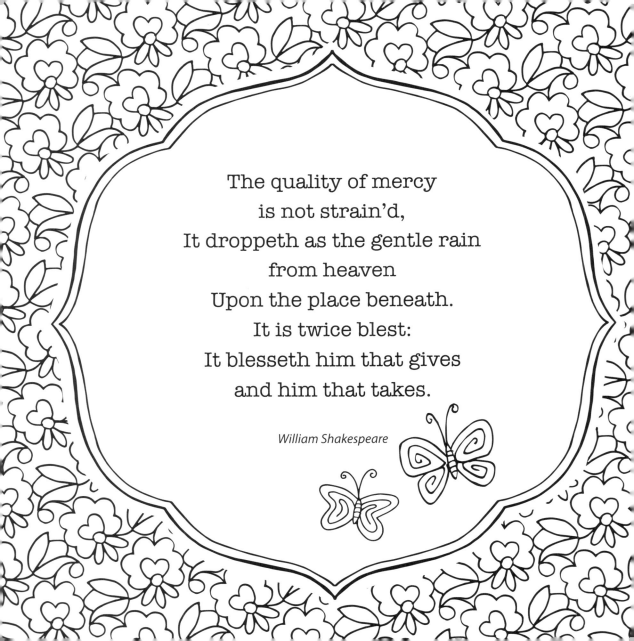

The quality of mercy
is not strain'd,
It droppeth as the gentle rain
from heaven
Upon the place beneath.
It is twice blest:
It blesseth him that gives
and him that takes.

William Shakespeare

grace

Gentle rain on a summer's day. In the garden, all dust is washed away and the world is sparkling and new. God's grace is like that: it washes away resentment and anger; shortcomings and guilt. I can live free as a butterfly.

WITH THE LORD THERE IS MERCY, AND WITH HIM IS PLENTEOUS REDEMPTION.

Psalm 130:7 (KJV)

May grace and peace be yours in full measure through your knowledge of God and of Jesus our LORD.

2 Peter 1:2 (GNB)

☆ What does grace mean to me?

....
....
....
....
....
....

☆ What role does forgiveness play in my life?

....
....
....
....
....
....

☆ How can I feel free?

....
....
....
....
....
....

☆ What would my life look like with grace and
peace in full measure?

....
....
....
....
....
....

May your choices reflect your hopes, not your fears.

Nelson Mandela

Freedom of choice

I want to choose what's right. I want to choose a life as God's beloved child. I want to choose what he asks of me: respect for others and self-respect. Joy, connectedness and trust. And I want to choose against fear, materialism and indifference. Every day I want to renew my choice. Every day I want to raise my hands and receive God's strength. This is what I choose.

Lift up your tired hands, then, and strengthen your trembling knees! Keep walking on straight paths, so that the lame foot may not be disabled, but instead be healed.

Hebrews 12:12–13 (GNB)

Rejoice in the Lord always.
I will say it again:
Rejoice!

Philippians 4:4

☆ What do I want to choose?

....

....

....

....

....

☆ What would that choice entail?

....

....

....

....

....

☆ What do I want to let go of?

....
....
....
....
....
....

☆ What can give me the strength to do so?

....
....
....
....
....
....

Three grand essentials to happiness in this life are something to do, something to love, and something to hope for.

Joseph Addison

Happiness

Whole nations look for it, fairytales end with it, Pharrell Williams sings about it: happiness. It is often powerful but fleeting – we have it, but soon lose it. I believe happiness is a byproduct. You don't get it by running after it, but by focusing on other things: God, faithful love, a meaningful way to spend the day, a life characterized by hope and trust.

There are many who say,
"Who will show us some good?
Lift up the light of your face upon us,
O Lord!"

Psalm 4:6 (ESV)

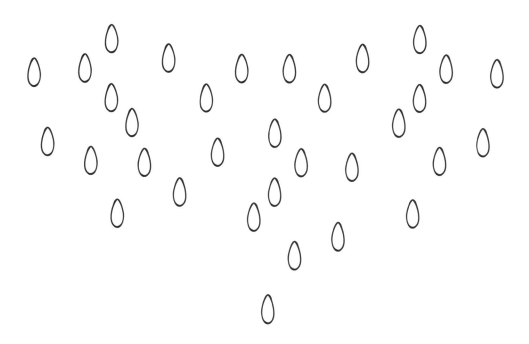

How happy are those
whose strength comes from you,
who are eager to make
the pilgrimage to Mount Zion.
As they pass through the dry valley of Baca,
it becomes a place of springs,
the autumn rain fills it with pools.

Psalm 84:5–6

☆ When did I feel very happy?

....

....

....

....

....

....

☆ What are the basic requirements for me to be happy?

....

....

....

....

....

....

☆ What do I want to focus on?

....
....
....
....
....
....

☆ What does it mean to seek your happiness in the Lord?

....
....
....
....
....
....

Prayer is more than meditation. In meditation, the source of strength is one's self. When one prays, he goes to a source of strength greater than his own.

Madame de Stael

strength

I need strength. All the time. Strength to say "no" to what is not right. Strength to keep going. Strength to thrive. I don't always think about it, but that strength is always available, at the Source.

For the Spirit that God has given us does not make us timid; instead, his Spirit fills us with power, love, and self-control.

2 Timothy 1:7

Now to him who is able to do
immeasurably more than all we ask
or imagine, according to his power
that is at work within us, to him be
glory in the church and in Christ Jesus
throughout all generations, for ever
and ever! Amen.

Ephesians 3:20-21

⭐ What do I need strength for?

....

....

....

....

....

....

⭐ What is my prayer?

....

....

....

....

....

....

☆ What gives me the strength to thrive?

....
....
....
....
....
....

☆ For what have I received strength?

....
....
....
....
....
....

I found I had less and less to say, until finally, I became silent, and began to listen. I discovered in the silence, the voice of God.

Søren Kierkegaard

silence

We live in a time filled with sounds, with sensory input. WhatsApp messages, telephone calls, thumping music in the gym, muzak in the supermarket, murmuring traffic – silence is rare in my life.

But though I long for silence, it always takes me a while to muster the courage to switch off my telephone, tablet and TV. Too afraid to miss out. But doesn't all that sound mean I miss out on something more important?

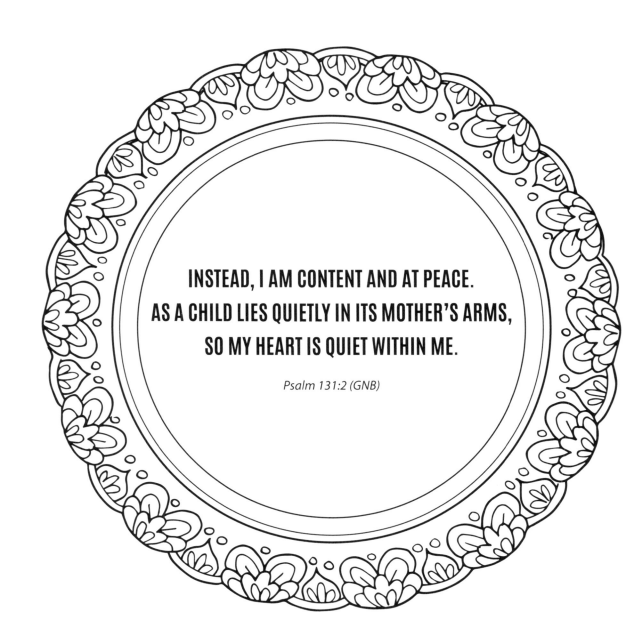

INSTEAD, I AM CONTENT AND AT PEACE.
AS A CHILD LIES QUIETLY IN ITS MOTHER'S ARMS,
SO MY HEART IS QUIET WITHIN ME.

Psalm 131:2 (GNB)

The Lord is my shepherd.
I have everything I need.
He lets me rest in fields
of green grass
and leads me to quiet pools
of fresh water.
He gives me new strength.

He guides me,
in the right paths
as he has promised.

Psalm 23:1-3 (GNB)

☆ What makes it difficult for me to experience silence?

....
....
....
....
....
....

☆ What have I missed in all the hustle and bustle of my life?

....
....
....
....
....
....

☆ How can I find silence in my life?

....
....
....
....
....
....

☆ What is my most precious experience of silence?

....
....
....
....
....
....

I arise today,
through God's strength to pilot me:
God's might to uphold me,
God's wisdom to guide me,
God's eye to look before me,
God's ear to hear me,
God's word to speak for me,
God's hand to guard me,
God's way to lie before me,
God's shield to protect me.
Christ with me,
Christ before me,
Christ behind me,
Christ in me,
Christ beneath me,
Christ above me,
Christ on my right,

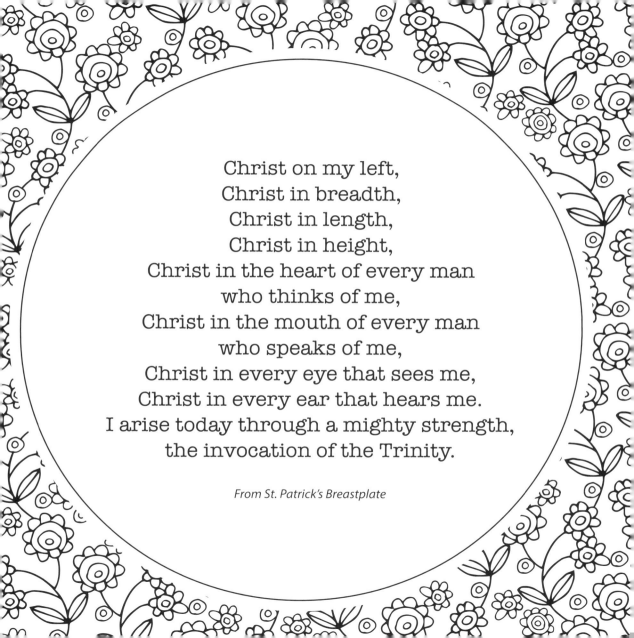

Christ on my left,
Christ in breadth,
Christ in length,
Christ in height,
Christ in the heart of every man
who thinks of me,
Christ in the mouth of every man
who speaks of me,
Christ in every eye that sees me,
Christ in every ear that hears me.
I arise today through a mighty strength,
the invocation of the Trinity.

From St. Patrick's Breastplate